Ta Mi Bida!

It's My Life!

By

Thamara Angel-Erdelyi

Introduction

It makes me sad to see how many women with so much potential settle for less. They stay in toxic relationships for years and lose themselves in the process. We, as women are so powerful and resourceful, but sometimes, or many times, we don't believe this. We stay in our comfort zone, even if this comfort zone is bad for us. We expect very little, and we are okay with leftovers and breadcrumbs.

There are many reasons why we do this. The number one reason is fear and the second is lack of self-confidence and self-love. On top of that women tend to be people pleasers. We are encouraged from the get-go to be complacent and please everybody and in that process, we forget (about) ourselves.

"Oh, you are such a sweet, good girl" was babbled into our heads for years and so we became the sweet compliant girls.

This compliance used to serve us to get and stay out of trouble at some point. To get positive attention. But growing up is a different ball game.

You cannot be a sweet and a good girl in the face of disrespect, abuse, or any form of harm towards you.

In this book I will tell you my story and what I have experienced and give you some tools and my knowledge to help you stand up for yourself, get that inner strength back and to live a life aligned to who you truly are.

This book is for women that are struggling in a toxic relationship and don't know how to get out. I think you can use this book also if you struggle with any type of toxic relationship. Not only with a spouse, partner but also any toxic relationship that you might have with a family member, with a friend or with a colleague at work. Of course, the intensity of the bond with a colleague is less than with your spouse. But the lessons in this book can help you anywhere in life.

Who is Thamara?

Through the years 2007-2012, I was in a toxic relationship. Back then I was only 27. It was one in which infidelity, mental, and emotional abuse ran amok. Finally, it also became physical.

I was young and in love and I always thought to myself, "he's going to change" and I stayed almost 5 years. But he didn't change, and I had to move out.

Was it easy? H$%# NO! But in this book, I will give you my life's experience, some tools, and the knowledge I have as a Coach. With this combination I think and hope I can help you be more aware of your situation. You cannot change what you don't know. Definitely, this ought to be the first step in any change. After awareness comes action and a diligent willingness to work on yourself to regain back your strengths and self-worth!

What are you going to learn?

In the first chapter I will tell you about my story and in the 2nd chapter I will explain what a toxic relationship is.

In the 3rd chapter I will tell my story of how I left, and my own formula called L.E.A.P. Chapter 4 explains the red flags. Chapter 5 is an important chapter about getting out of the comfort zone and dealing with fears and doubts. Chapter 6 is how to really jump out of that bad toxic relationship. After you leave come feelings of guilt. I will tackle this in chapter 7. In chapter 8, I will explain the healing process. Chapter 9 is about self-discovery. How to find yourself, after you've lost yourself in the relationship. After this, in Chapter 10, I look at how to regain self-confidence and self-love. Chapter 11 is about living in alignment to who you truly are. And the last chapter is about finding your purpose, your meaning in life (Ikigai).

I really hope that this book will inspire you and to give you some tools. I hope my mess back then can be a message for you today. And now without further ado let's jump into chapter 1.

Table of Contents

Ta Mi Bida!

Chapter 1 - The Theme Park

I was 26 years old, young and I had just finished my degree in Education. I came back to Curaçao because I had been studying in Holland. After I had been back for a few months I met this handsome man. He was fine and he was lean and slim and very charming. I fell in love immediately. The days passed and we got to know each other better. We fell madly in love. I was the most beautiful girl for him, and he adored me. He was a gentleman. He opened the car-door for me. I always felt protected. He even gave me some money when I needed, which although this was not something I wanted to accept, I did.

From there we started living together and the first year was great! The relationship was passionate. Yes, read that again. Because that's what it was, only passionate. This relationship wasn't based on good communication, trust, or any basic needs of a relationship. It was based on a passionate, sexual life. Because let's be honest, that was very good at that point. But the rest was lacking.

1

The more I wanted the other stuff like attention, quality time, and communication, seeing that those things really matter to a woman, he started pulling away. It was just like I was pushing him away by asking for these things. He went on doing more sports, working many hours because his work was so demanding. He acted as if his life depended on that job and couldn't say no to anything. But every time he was saying yes to his job he was saying "no" to me. Of course he had to work, but it was more about every happy hour and every lunch meeting he had to attend, and working so many extra hours, that was really bothering me. The more I told him to be at home and that I needed and missed him, to him I was nagging and complaining.

His answer was always that he needed to work, and he had to do sports. Mind you, every day!!! I asked him if he could skip 1 night out of the 7 days so he could be at home and help me out. He would then argue with me and would get very aggressive about not leaving his sports for me.

He used to come home at 8, but then every day that became later, 8:30, 9:00, 9:30, 10:00 o'clock. But, hey, I was the one nagging again. He started to get more aggressive and unresponsive when I would call him. His phone was shut off, and I couldn't communicate with him. That made me anxious, and I started having anxiety attacks at home.

Then a child came into the relationship. I got pregnant, and for a few months it was fun, and he helped a bit. But then soon enough everything became overwhelming for him, I suppose, so he became very absent again. You best believe that he never skipped a day of doing sports. He thus only saw our child in the mornings. Even when I pleaded with him to help me out one day of the week with the night routine, he wasn't willing.

I had this weird feeling that something was off. He wasn't paying attention at all to either of us. He wasn't answering his phone when I needed him.

We argued a lot. After each argument he would give me the silent treatment like I didn't exist. But after a few days having an argument, we would have sex. And just like that we 'made up'. And this cycle continued like this. There was no communication about what happened in the argument or how we could solve this for the future so that it wouldn't happen again.

I suspected him of cheating, but I couldn't put my finger on it. Until much later.

When I found out, I forgave him, because he was sorry, and I loved him so much. You might think "how stupid of you". But when you are blinded by love and you really think he is the best thing since sliced bread, you stick with it.

So, we continued for five more years.

After all the emotional and mental abuse, the physical abuse began. He only did this twice. Twice, is two too many.

Once he pushed me against the door when I was pregnant, and he held me by the throat. This was a surreal moment. Did he really do this? I stood there and I couldn't move. I froze. And I thought to myself, "don't you see I'm pregnant with your child?" At that moment he was clueless of this fact that he could hurt me and the baby. I felt an incredible sadness in me. I wasn't scared. I was sad and so disappointed.

The 2nd time he pushed me, and I fell on a table. From the table I fell on the ground. When I was on the ground, he sat on me and he held me by the throat again, like he wanted to choke me. He didn't squeeze, yet!

Then my "psychologist mind" started working and I thought in a few split seconds, what could I possible say at that moment to make him rethink? There was no time for fear or any other feeling, but it was a survival mode that kicked in. And I started talking him out of it, by saying to him remember your children, remember your children. Like maybe that would help to get him out of that stage or the idea to squeeze my throat and with all the consequences of it. He then miraculously let go and he left. I laid there on the floor in disbelief, and I was so empty. I couldn't feel anything. I was numb.

After laying there a few minutes, I stood up and went to the fridge to get some water. While standing there facing the fridge, I saw a picture I had put there of me and my daughter. And I can remember very clear the question that I asked myself: "Do you want to stay in this s#@$ for 30 more years?" And the answer was a loud and clear "NO".

At that moment I decided I would leave. In the meantime, he returned home. It was evening and I was already in my pajamas. When he went in the room, I thought, I must leave now!

I took my daughter; she was about 2 years old back then. I put her in the car, and I told him I was going to buy gas or electricity I don't even remember anymore. He didn't even react.

So, I left……

As I mentioned, this cycle went on for about 5 years that I was with him. Every time we split up; I would go back. This game of pushing and pulling felt like a roller coaster ride of emotions. But I guess I liked it. Because for some strange reason it kept everything so excited, and life wasn't boring. It wasn't healthy, but at least it wasn't boring.

This cycle continued, until that very day in the kitchen. At that moment I made a conscious decision to leave this 'theme park' and all its roller coaster rides.

Chapter 2 - What is a Toxic Relationship?

After I left, I understood that I had been in a toxic relationship. I didn't know it at that time.

But what is a toxic relationship?

There is an abundance of research on this topic. Dr. Lilian Glass, a California-based communication and psychology expert, defines a toxic relationship as "any relationship (between people who) don't support each other, where there's conflict and one seek to undermine the other, where there's competition, where there's disrespect and a lack of cohesiveness."

While every relationship goes through ups and downs, Glass claims a toxic relationship is consistently unpleasant and draining for the people in it, to the point that negative moments outweigh and outnumber the positive ones. Dr. Kristen Fuller, a California-based family medicine physician who specializes in mental health, adds that toxic relationships are mentally, emotionally, and possibly even physically damaging to one or both participants.

These relationships don't have to be romantic: Glass says friendly, familial, and professional relationships can all be toxic as well.

https://e-psychotherapy.com/toxic-relationships/?cli_action=1630574375.028

What makes a relationship toxic?

Fuller says people who consistently undermine or cause harm to a partner — whether intentionally or not — often have a reason for their behavior, even if it's subconscious. "Maybe they were in a toxic relationship, either romantically or as a child. Maybe they didn't have the most supportive, loving upbringing," Fuller says. "They could have been bullied in school. They could be suffering from an undiagnosed mental health disorder, such as depression or anxiety or bipolar disorder, an eating disorder, any form of trauma."

What are the warning signs of a toxic relationship?

The most serious warning signs include any form of violence, abuse, or harassment, which should be dealt with immediately. But in many cases, the indicators of a toxic relationship are much more subtle.

The first, and simplest, is persistent unhappiness, Glass says. If a relationship stops bringing joy, and instead consistently makes you feel sad, angry, and anxious or "resigned, like you've sold out," it may be toxic,

Glass says. You may also find yourself envious of happy couples.

Fuller says negative shifts in your mental health, personality or self-esteem are all red flags, too. These changes could range from clinically diagnosable conditions, such as depression, anxiety or eating disorders, to constantly feeling nervous or uncomfortable — especially around your partner. Feeling like you can't talk with or voice concerns to your significant other is another sign that something is amiss, Fuller says.

You should also look out for changes in your other relationships, or in the ways you spend your free time, Fuller says. "You may feel bad for doing things on your own time, because you feel like you have to attend to your partner all the time," she says. "You cross the line when you're not your individual self anymore and you're giving everything to your partner."

People in a toxic relationship often are the ones that are the last to realize that they are in such a relationship.

https://time.com/5274206/toxic-relationship-signs-help/

Here are some signs to look out for when assessing whether you are in a toxic or harmful relationship:

- You don't feel good enough. You feel like nothing you do is quite right and are constantly trying to prove your worth. You constantly seek the other person's validation.

- You can't be yourself. You feel you have to walk on eggshells and monitor everything you say and do. You feel you need to think twice before you speak as certain topics are off limits, and you feel you have to act or behave a certain way. You're afraid to bring things up because you're not sure how the other person will react.

- The other person puts you down.

- You feel like the problem. The other person doesn't take responsibility for their actions and instead blames you. They attribute any problems or difficulties in the relationship as all your fault.

- You start to withdraw from participating in activities or seeing people in your life.

https://e-psychotherapy.com/toxic-relationships/?cli_action=1630574375.028

My Findings/ discoveries

By the time I realized that I was in a toxic relationship and that it was unhealthy for me, it was so normal to me that it didn't seem like that big of a deal. You are so used to it, that you are paralyzed by it.

After I left, I started to analyze myself. I had moments that I was sleeping constantly. This could be a sign of depression. But back then I didn't know. I felt anxious at times and had anxiety attacks when I couldn't reach him. I was losing contact with my friends and family, because I didn't want to leave and do things for myself, because I thought I had to tend to him all the time. I also felt nervous around him sometimes and to speak up for myself was a NO-GO, otherwise this would have ended in an ugly argument.

I couldn't be myself. I was a prisoner in my own house. What should you do if you're in a toxic relationship? If any of those red flags sound familiar, it's time to take action. I will speak more on the red flags in chapter 4. But first I will tell you how I left and maybe my experience can help you leave too.

Chapter 3 - The L.E.A.P.

From my point of view, a toxic relationship is an unstable relationship where you cannot rely on the other person. He/she is emotionally unavailable, he/she does things and then blames you for his/her bad behavior, like it was your fault that he/she did this or that. It is a co-dependency where you think you cannot live without him. But even though sometimes it's horrible, sometimes it's great. We do have our happy moments, right? Or not? I don't remember. I loved him and I didn't want to break up with him. I loved him more than myself. Haaaaaa more on this later.

What it does with your self-esteem…. pffffft what is that? Self-esteem??? At that point in time, I couldn't even recognize myself. I was less than the doormat at the front door. That's how I was feeling. After the cheating, I went crazy thinking and comparing myself with the other woman. I was tired, looking bad, I had black circles and bags under my eyes. I didn't realize it much at that time. A few months after having left, a very good friend of mine told me how she saw me and how I looked. I can imagine I looked like Frankenstein or Morticia Addams. And don't take me wrong, Morticia is a beautiful woman, but those black eyes were not from make-up. You get my point?

To come back to the point where I decided to leave, I had no self-esteem, no self-love, and no self-respect. But I left! And as I look back, I think this was very courageous. I had no self-anything but I least I was brave!!! And so are you!!!

If there is one inch in your soul that is courageous and you can have one more breath in you, leave! You will be okay, I guarantee you. Not only okay, but you will be relieved and so much happier.

The one thing that also helped me to take the decision was my daughter. Did I want her to see me like this? Did I want her to be raised in this type of household? She would think this was normal. As an educator, I knew darn right that this wasn't a safe environment in which to raise any kid.

So, I took the LEAP.

Sitting in the car with my daughter, leaving through the front gate, as the automatic gate was opening, I felt very, very sad. I felt an emptiness inside. Trying to hold back my tears, so that my daughter sitting in the back seat, wouldn't notice much. It felt like "my world" was crashing down. I felt like a failure. As the gate opened and I drove towards the street, leaving my home behind I couldn't hold back my tears anymore. I cried like a baby. I felt like my heart had been ripped out of my body. It literally hurt. I don't mean like a figure of speech, but literally like when you hurt your foot and you feel pain. Just like that. I really felt physical pain in my chest. As I drove to my mother's house, I turned around many times to see how my daughter was. At first, she was playing with a doll, and after a while she fell asleep.

I arrived at my mom's house. Devastated! Broken to pieces! In my PJ's, Hahahaha, remember?

Now what??? What now?

I was merely a body, sleepwalking like a ghost. With a broken heart and a daughter to raise on my own.

My mother, may her soul rest in peace, took us inside the house. I couldn't remember much of what happened that day. I think I slept the whole day. While my mom entertained the little one. Oh, she loved her!!! She was happy we were there. Thinking back, it makes me miss my mom even more.

After this 'beauty sleep' that was feeling like a combination of Snow White (half dead) and Sleeping beauty. The one that was hurt by the spindle of a spinning wheel and then fell into a deep sleep, which was really a curse put on her by Maleficent who tricked her into pricking herself.

Aha! Something confusing like that. I was feeling like a combination of these 2. Is that even possible? I don't know but I felt like that.

And then miraculously I woke up. To my new life. That I didn't even know existed nor did I know how I was going to live it or make it on my own. The strength that I had left was to fight for my daughter. She had to live and be everything I wasn't at that time. I thought: "I will teach this little girl how to stand up in life and never ever let anyone or anything put her down." How would I do this? I didn't know at that moment. But that very thought, was both my strength and my salvation.

I took the "L.E.A.P.". And I made this up; the L.E.A.P. stands for 'Love yourself', 'Exit', 'Accept help', 'Promise' yourself you will never go back to where they hurt you.

So please take the LEAP!

Chapter 4 - Red Flags

What can I say about red flags? These are signs that you see at the beginning of a relationship, but you ignore. Like any aggressive, manipulative behavior. Or something he/she does that is fishy in any way.

But because we are blinded by "love," we make up excuses for this behavior and we squelch it.

I remember once we went to a night club and when we were leaving the club, a stranger called out to me with a "hey beautiful". He was drunk and he just said it without meaning any harm as he continued walking. He wasn't harassing me.

Well at that moment, my ex became like the Hulk in the movie. The drunk guy jumped in his car to drive away, but my ex went after him and slammed his fist aggressively on the roof of the car leaving a dent.

I stood there in shock, and I really didn't know what to do. And there were some other people standing around the parking lot, looking at this whole scene. I felt very bad and embarrassed.

He then came with the story that he wanted to protect me, and that nobody had the right to talk to me like that in such a disrespectful way. He wanted to be the hero. Instead, I felt he was a horrible creature that I didn't recognize.

The next day he came with the excuse that he acted that way because he was drunk, but he never said that he really felt sorry for what he had done.

Another time we went to a Christmas party, and I bumped into my ex-boyfriend. My ex-boyfriend came over to greet me with a hug and a kiss. At that moment my ex exploded with rage. He was furious. They started quarrelling and the security guy came along and told him he had to leave the party. You can just imagine how embarrassed I was. All my friends were at the party. I really felt I could die at that moment. I wished the earth would open and swallow me.

Why do we ignore these red flags? Are we not assertive enough? Or do we see them, but we ignore them anyway?

In my case, he would always have an explanation for why he did certain things, and it was always because he supposedly loved me so much and he wanted to protect me, and nobody was allowed to disrespect me.

I thought it was cute, that he wanted to protect me. He was my hero, right? Well, I didn't really know how heroes should behave. After his explanation, I always thought: "it wasn't that bad after all". He just wanted to protect me. He's being jealous.

Speaking of jealousy. This dude was so jealous that no man could say hello to me or really say anything to me. Besides, I'm a very social and talkative person. Can you imagine how I felt? I felt imprisoned.

I slowly but surely entered my shield. I didn't want any guy to look at me or greet me, because then we would have problems.

The bubbly person I once was, started to become an introverted girl walking under a grey cloud. I allowed him to push me behind my shield. And by then I couldn't recognize myself. I lost myself, my personality, my identity, my self-confidence, and myself.

Ta Mi Bida!

Chapter 5 - Stepping out of that "bad" comfort zone

Fear is the number one thing that paralyzes people. We let fear get the best of us. So many times, when we are in a bad situation, we stay, because we convince ourselves that it's not that bad after all. And who knows what's out there? It could be much worse than your current situation, right? We stay in that comfort zone, which is bad for us, but we stay there because we think there is a ring of fire around this comfort zone and that we will burn if we step outside of it. In the meantime, we are burning alive inside that ring of fire.

We forget to think for ourselves. We forget that we have options. We are so conditioned in this comfort zone.

I stayed out of fear and because I still loved him. Yes, can you imagine!? Fear of being alone. Would I ever find another partner? Fear of the outside world. I thought it could be worse than the current one. Fear of raising my daughter alone. Fear of the unknown.

Do you have these fears too?

If you want to step out of your comfort zone, you must stretch and think in possibilities. What if outside is better? What would it look like? I think I could do this with the help and support of others. You have to think positive and affirming thoughts. These thoughts can help you to give you strength and courage to confront the fears and step out.

Whether you think you can do something or not, both you are right. It all starts in the mind.

It's a mindset shift. Remember you are not your fears. And you have everything in you, you a resourceful, to continue your life on your own. And no, you won't be alone! You have people around you that love you.

What is this 'suspicious' comfort zone that everybody talks about?

It's the zone that you are living in. This area of your life you are familiar with, it feels safe. Your habits, your behavior is all so automated. You live in this zone without thinking much. Your brain always wants to conserve energy. Because your brain has made some pathways (like highways and byways) and these pathways manage your life.

As soon as you want to do something new, or you want to install a new habit? Your brain goes…………NOOOOO STOP. Don't! Dinosaurs are running behind you. That's how you feel. Dinosaurs that are going to kill you. You are in fight or flight mode. And so many times or most of the time the "flight" mode wins. You don't fight and you settle for less.

The negative thoughts kick in and you tell yourself all the ways that you can't do it. You don't even try to fight for the great things you want. Or you stay stuck in a bad situation or environment.

Why do we let fear win most of the time? It's not even your fault. Really! Our brain has developed over the years. But there is part of it that is very old. This part of the brain is pre-historic and used to serve us well during "cave time". Where we would have been eaten alive by Dino's or saber-toothed tigers. The fight or flight instinct then kicked in, so we could survive these dangers.

Now fast forward to the 21st century where there are no more dinosaurs. Okay, let's be clear here, there are spiders and cockroaches, these are also very scary just like dinosaurs. But you get my point, right?

Our fight or flight mode kicks in every time we want to do something new. Or when we want to step out of the comfort zone, do something unusual or leave a complacent place, relationship, or career. The side effects of that fear are the same as if your life is in danger. Your brain doesn't really know at that moment in time that you are in a life-threatening situation or that you just want to quit your dissatisfying job. Or you want to step out of a bad relationship. Or even learn a new skill. This makes people sweat, shake and get really nervous as well. For example, when we needed to learn how to work with the online Zoom program. I for sure felt Dinosaurs running after me. Nonetheless, I learned how to use it and I don't feel anxious anymore.

This means that a bad situation can also be your comfort zone. Yes, even if it's bad, harmful, or painful. Because your belief system tells you many lies. Like you better stay here, because you really don't know what's out there. There are worse men than this one. I don't think I can raise a child on my own. I don't have enough money on my own. Well after all, you might think: "this situation isn't that bad after all". Your brain fabricates all these excuses and excuses for all the bad things.

I hear so many times people saying they don't like their jobs. And then they tell themselves all the reasons they should stay. "Well, it isn't easy to get a job these days with the pandemic". "Jobs are limited". "I don't like my job but at least I have a job". "So many people don't have a job". "It could be worse".

Guys let me tell you this! I did quit my permanent job in the year 2020 during the first lockdown. I decided I didn't want to go back to work at a school. Not because I didn't like it, on the contrary, I loved my students, but there was something missing. I needed more room for my creative ideas and my true passion.

What were you thinking??? So many people told me, "Are you crazy? People are losing jobs now, and you quit your permanent job?" Yes, I did!

You know why? Because there is never a good time!!!!!! Back then it was COVID 19, maybe this year it will be COVID 20 and next year would be COVID 21. Do I want to live 3 more years just 'surviving' and not really thriving? The answer was no.

If you wait for the perfect timing and the perfect circumstances, then you'll have a lot of waiting to do my friend.

There is no such thing as the perfect time.

Do you need a plan B? I think so, but you don't need to have everything figured out before you take the leap. More on this in the chapter about preparing your parachute. I sometimes think just like Cortez "El Conquistador". When he arrived at an unknown island, he told his people: "burn the boats". Why did he do that? Because he was willing to confront everything on that island to conquer it. No turning back!!! I'm like Cortez. Sometimes you must burn your boats and not look back. Only looking forward on how to conquer "your" island.

5.1 How to confront these fears.

To confront any fear in life you first have to be aware of your fears. You can be aware by writing them down. Then you have to acknowledge them. Ok I'm fearful because……………and you fill it in. Then you have to embrace it. You have to welcome it and follow through. Fear is not a stop sign. In any situation that is unknown, whenever you are just stepping out of your comfort zone, fear kicks in. It's ok and it's normal. Then you have to think critically about the thought behind your fears. Is it true? Is it helpful? Ask yourself these questions when you have written down the thoughts and/or the feelings.

Befriend your fears. Because what you resist persists. What you befriend, transcends. This I learned from the great author Robin Sharma.

Our fears form a wall if we don't deal with them. And before you know it, you have the whole Great Wall of China rebuilt around you all over again. We need to break these walls down.

And you know what? The more you confront your fears and do the things you should do anyway, every time it will be easier to deal with fears and follow through. Will the fears become less? Well, some fears that you overcome won't feel as bad after a few times you've done the things you should have done. But your brain is really a creep sometimes. When you have dealt with some of the voices in your head (no you are not delusional, these voices are the negative thoughts and self-talk and self-doubt we have), other voices arise.

Let me explain. For example, we were forced to do meetings online because of the lockdown, therefore you had to go online with the program Microsoft Teams. I had to deal with the voices that told me "you're not really a high-tech person, it will take you forever to learn this Team thing". "OMG, I don't like anything online etc." When you've dealt with all of these, you will feel more at ease going online. But then something happens, and you cannot use Teams anymore, you have to use Zoom instead. Now some new voices arise. "You were good at Teams and now you have to learn a new program. What is this Zoom anyway? I can't learn two different programs to go online. It took me so much time to learn Teams and now I need to learn Zoom. I don't have time."

The voices in your head won't go away completely. The old voices will fade and some new voices will arise. But in my experience, the voices are not as loud as they were in the beginning, and I was able to deal with them easier and smarter. I go through these steps much them faster every time. Because I know how it works. And so can you! These steps are:

1. Be aware of the voices. The negative thoughts, self-doubt, etc.

2. Write them down in your journal.

3. Acknowledge them. Okay, I see you, come sit next to me.

4. Befriend your fears.

5. Question your thoughts. Be critical about them. Like in the example. Is it true that I cannot learn two online programs?

6. Take the leap anyways with fear. Do it afraid!!!! That's my motto!

Remember courage is not the absence of fear. It's doing the thing you are afraid to do while you are afraid.

5.2 How can you have this inner strength to step out?

If you are in a bad situation, a toxic relationship, and you've been mental, emotionally, or physically abused, you probably don't have much self-esteem and self-love left. I can tell you my story and what I did. For me it was one decision. I didn't want to live like this for the next 30 to 40 years.

Ask yourself the same question. And if the answer is NO, then you must leave! He is not going to change and NO that is not love. A toxic relationship is not healthy, and the other person must find psychological help. But that's another story. We are focusing on you now.

How to leave? Look for a support system. Your parents, friends, or any family member.

The second most important thing after the decision to leave is that you need to have courage. Take it from me, you will be fine. Better than fine, you will be happy when you leave. Take it from me and thousands of other women who have left a toxic relationship.

If you think back on your childhood when you used to be courageous and you undertook some courageous endeavors back then, it means that it is still in you, and you have the courage to leave.

Love yourself dear sister, even if you don't love yourself enough, start saying to yourself "I am enough". Say it every day until you start believing this.

5.3. Limiting beliefs and negative thoughts.

We all have some deep-rooted limiting beliefs and negative thoughts in us. Let me explain the difference. Beliefs are like agreements, standards we believe are true and so it is. For example, I'm not creative, I'm not good at technology, I suck at sports, I'm a bad cook, etc. etc. Most of these beliefs come from an experience in the past, something we heard, saw, or experienced. And we took these things as "truths" and we believed them and made them part of our identity. So whenever there is a painting class or a crochet class, the first things that pops up in your mind is "I'm not creative" and then you don't register for the class. Because it reminds you that you are not creative.

In the past, I used to tell myself this. Until I realized it was a limiting belief. I then started to say to myself that I can learn anything and that I'm creative in so many ways. Another limiting belief of mine is that I suck at sports. By asking yourself the question, "when did I come up with this belief? You force yourself to dig a deep into your child- and young adulthood.

I remember during high school we had to run 10 circles around the block, and I couldn't do it. My condition and endurance weren't that good. For every round you would get 1 point. therefore, after 6 rounds, you would score a 6 and after 9 rounds you would score a 9. Zero was very bad off course and 10 was excellent.

I remember the day before I told my mom I didn't want to go to school. I was dreading this day. Anyway, I had to go to school, and I ran only 5 rounds. I almost died in the process, and I was laughed at by my classmates. How is it possible you couldn't run more than 5 rounds? They couldn't believe that I was that weak.

From that day on, I internalized the "I suck at sports" belief. Do you see how this works??

Little did I know, years later when I was pregnant, I had to go to the cardiologist. Where he saw through an ECG that I had a "hole" or a leakage in my heart. This meant I could get an infection easier than others and that I tire more easily than others.

Ahhhhhhaaaaaaaaaaaaaaaaaaaaaaaaaaaaaaaaaaaa aaaaaaaaaaaaaaaaaaaaaaa!!!!!! What an AHA moment! This explained a lot. I didn't suck at sports, I just got tired much faster than others. I wished I could go back and tell the gym teacher this, who wasn't very nice to me nor to my classmates. But whatever! It is what it is.

But this belief, haunted me all my life. And at 40 I'm trying to tell myself that sports can be fun. I'm trying to change that belief. But it's not easy to change a belief, but it's also not impossible.

Now let's look at negative thoughts. A negative thought is a thought that shows up sometimes in your mind. When you have to do something, but you are scared, you can have thoughts like: "Can I do this, maybe I can't". "I'm not good enough", "Nobody is paying me for this workshop", "maybe I won't get clients" and with this book I thought: "would anybody buy it?"

It is easier to work on a negative thought than a belief. But you have to be very aware of your thoughts. Whenever a negative thought crosses your mind, you need to ask yourself this question: Is what I'm thinking really true?

We have so many unconscious thoughts that we are not aware of. Did you know that 95% of our thoughts are unconscious? And that only 3-5 % are conscious! What does this mean? We do everything: our habits, our behavior, decisions we make mostly on automatic pilot.

A good tool is to journal about your thoughts. And then you can read them out loud and be critical about what you read. Don't believe everything your mind tells you and for sure if it's negative.

5.4. The Dinosaur Slayer

Before I left that very last day and didn't come back, we broke up several times before. And twice I left for a few days and then came back after pleading from his side. I fell back into that comfort zone twice. Because it was familiar and, hey remember, I loved him a lot. But let me tell you this. NOTHING, and I mean NOTHING changed. It was all promises and lies, like the UB40 song. And that love wasn't love at all. It was an unhealthy co-dependency where there was no respect and no communication.

Now, why do we return so easily to our comfort zones even if the situation is bad? It sounds crazy but your mind tricks you into believing that whatever is outside of that comfort zone could be worse. Can you imagine outside there, there could be a guy worse than this one. And let's be honest here. This guy isn't that bad. He has good traits, he's a hard-working guy, responsible at work, he pays the bills, or well 50%, and we don't always fight. Well okay, sometimes he doesn't speak to me for days, giving me the silent treatment. Well at least then we don't fight.

Our comfort zone is the place of familiarity, a place we feel safe somehow, even though it's a bad situation or environment.

What brought me back twice is also the fact that I hoped things would change. And I thought of our family. I didn't want to be the one who would break up the family. And I really loved him a lot still. But nothing changed.

The challenge is to do something you want to do even if you have fears and negative thoughts. Believe me, when you stretch yourself a bit, the thing that once was difficult will become easier. But then you have to stretch yourself a bit more. And then the same scary scene will appear again with the dinosaurs chasing after you like a real-life Jurassic Park. Oh, and the scary creatures take various forms. Today it could be a Dinosaur and tomorrow it can be a weird little creepy man that tells you why you shouldn't be doing something new, a new challenge. NO, you are not hallucinating, and you don't need to go to a psychiatrist, yet! These voices or thoughts are all created by our minds. And you need to think like this: I am not my thoughts. Question your thoughts.

If you start seeing a dinosaur in your house or if you see that little creepy man in front of you and you start having a conversation with them and they speak back to you, then you might look for help with a psychiatrist. Because than the situation is a bit more serious.

But really all jokes set aside. If you push through, believe me, it's wonderful outside your comfort zone. You don' know what you are capable of doing if you don't stretch yourself. I encourage you to do so. If you need help and support, look for a mindset coach. You can always call me. I am the dinosaur slayer!

Chapter 6 - Prepare the Parachute

In April 2012, I was fed up. After almost 5 years of arguments, infidelity, verbal, and mental aggression. I was done, so done! When did I let this go so far? When did I permit somebody do these things to me? On that April evening, standing in my kitchen looking at the picture of me and my daughter, I decided that this was it! I was done suffering and I was not going to take this s&%# anymore.

That day I took my daughter, in my PJ's, and I left. That was the day the old "ME" died and I decided I wanted to find myself back. Later in this book I will continue about that topic.

There is a beautiful quote that says: "Part of you must die, for your greatness to emerge". And so it was. It was the best decision I could make in that moment.

How many times we hold on to these "old things" that don't serve us? Because we are afraid of letting go of things, we think we cannot let go. Because it has become a part of our identity. But if you can lose those things and find yourself and be more authentic, you will see great things happening in your life. You are then becoming the person you are supposed to be.

As my big guru Tony Robbins says: "Life happens for you, not to you." This is a quote that changed the way I look at life. The bad things that happen to you are necessary to form and build you. Without these bad experiences you wouldn't have become the person you are today. Let me give you my life's example. If this didn't happen to me, I wouldn't know how to set any boundaries, I wouldn't have become resilient and I wouldn't know to stand up for myself.

If you are still doubting what to do, believe me he is not going to change. You must go. Go sister, go!!!! Like in the movie, Go Forest, Go! From the movie Forest Gumb. Did you watch it? Well anyways back to you.

Please do yourself a favor and leave. Love and respect yourself. You are enough and you deserve more than this. Making this tough decision isn't easy but NOT making any decision at all, is lethal.

Find help, find support. Look for people that loves you and can help you get out. It's difficult to leave when you are alone. But it's not impossible. Look for a good friend or a family member to help you. If you don't have anybody, which I doubt, even a stranger with a good heart can and will help.

I was not alone, thank God. I had my mother. She was always there for me when I needed her, waiting for me.

I promise this! Everything outside of that 'bad comfort zone' is better than staying. And have faith and know that you are stronger than you think you are, and you can do this. You have everything in you, you are resourceful enough to handle this.

When you jump you also need to find professional help from a coach or a psychologist. You need to heal, sister. More on this later.

Finally, have faith my dear one, that you will be fine! And now let's see which color your parachute is? Did you prepare it? Is it good to go? Now count down with me!!! 5,4,3,2,1.....................Jump!

Ta Mi Bida!

Chapter 7 - Dealing with guilty feelings

After I left, the guilty feelings started arising. I was the one that broke up the family. I felt guilty at times. This guilty feeling is not any good. Firstly, you don't have to feel guilty because you didn't break up the family. Remember: He did!! Don't change the story or put any blame on you. Because of his behavior you were forced to leave. Sure, we all make mistakes. I made some too. I wasn't impeccable. I could have done some things differently. But I always tried to be nice to him, cook for him, clean the house, take care of the household, etc.

Blaming yourself is not helping you in any way. The sooner you can get over this, the better and faster the healing process can begin.

Sometimes we blame ourselves and on top of that others can also saddle us guilty feelings. They would say things like "oh he was such a nice guy, what happened?" I remember one family member told me: "Why do you always break up with the guys?" I was like huh? I only had like two relationships before this one. And now suddenly I'm the one breaking up every time?

Uhmmmmm…. DUH!!!!!!! I did. Because both were cheating on me and were disrespectful of me.

The truth is, nobody really knows what you are living or going through. NOBODY. And on top of that he had another version of how the things were. And of course, everybody in his family turned their backs on me. But after some time, believe me everybody will notice. So don't worry about telling everybody how things really were, you don't have to prove anything to anyone. Time will tell. By the way, here's a tip: read the book "The subtle art of not giving a F$%&". This book helped me a lot to not give too many f…. in a day about what people would think or say. They don't have a clue!

After some time, you fool yourself that "the relationship wasn't that bad", 'He was sweet at times". You then romanticize the good times, and you tend to forget about the bad things. Or you start lying to yourself that the bad things weren't that bad after all. It's like you are going back in your mind to your comfort zone and putting on your rose-colored glasses. It's like you are cleaning the hard disk of your mind, taking out cookies and viruses and you want to go back. STOP! Going back is and should not be an option.

We are going forward now. But this going forward is going to take some time and you will have to face some demons you have picked up along the way. We need to go through the hurt and pain so that you can really heal. How can you heal after this trauma of misuse and abuse? More on this in the coming chapter.

Ta Mi Bida!

Chapter 8 - The Healing Process

After the parachute jump, which left you feeling that you could have died in the process, the healing process starts. But first you have to grief. Grief is not only because somebody died, but grief comes also when you end a relationship.

Throughout life, we experience many instances of grief. Grief can be caused by situations, relationships, or even substance abuse. Children may grieve a divorce, a wife may grieve the death of her husband, a teenager might grieve the ending of a relationship, or you might have received terminal medical news and are grieving your pending death. In 1969, Elisabeth Kübler-Ross described five common stages of grief, popularly referred to as DABDA. They include:

- Denial
- Anger
- Bargaining
- Depression
- Acceptance

Denial

Denial is the stage that can initially help you survive the loss. You might think life makes no sense, has no meaning, and is too overwhelming. You start to deny the news and, in effect, go numb. It's common in this stage to wonder how life will go on in this different state – you are in a state of shock because life as you once knew it, has changed in an instant. If you were diagnosed with a deadly disease, you might believe the news is incorrect – a mistake must have occurred somewhere in the lab–they mixed up your blood work with someone else. If you receive news on the death of a loved one, perhaps you cling to a false hope that they identified the wrong person. In the denial stage, you are not living in 'actual reality,' rather, you are living in a 'preferable' reality. Interestingly, it is denial and shock that help you cope and survive the grief event. Denial aids in pacing your feelings of grief. Instead of becoming completely overwhelmed with grief, we deny it, do not accept it, and stagger its full impact on us at one time. Think of it as your body's natural defense mechanism saying "hey, there's only so much I can handle at once." Once the denial and shock starts to fade, the start of the healing process begins. At this point, those feelings that you were once suppressing are coming to the surface.

Anger

Once you start to live in 'actual' reality again and not in 'preferable' reality, anger might start to set in. This is a common stage to think "why me?" and "life's not fair!" You might look to blame others for the cause of your grief and also may redirect your anger to close friends and family. You find it incomprehensible of how something like this could happen to you. If you are strong in faith, you might start to question your belief in God. "Where is God? Why didn't he protect me?" Researchers and mental health professionals agree that this anger is a necessary stage of grief. And encourage the anger. It's important to truly feel the anger. It's thought that even though you might seem like you are in an endless cycle of anger, it will dissipate – and the more you truly feel the anger, the more quickly it will dissipate, and the more quickly you will heal. It is not healthy to suppress your feelings of anger – it is a natural response – and perhaps, arguably, a necessary one. In every day life, we are normally told to control our anger toward situations and toward others. When you experience a grief event, you might feel disconnected from reality – that you have no grounding anymore. Your life has shattered and there's nothing solid to hold onto. Think of anger as a strength to bind you to reality. You might feel deserted or abandoned during a grief event. That no one is there. You are alone in this world. The direction of anger toward something or somebody is what might bridge you back to reality and connect you to people again. It is a "thing." It's something to grasp onto – a natural step in healing.

Bargaining

When something bad happens, have you ever caught yourself making a deal with God? "Please God, if you heal my husband, I will strive to be the best wife I can ever be – and never complain again." This is bargaining. In a way, this stage is false hope. You might falsely make yourself believe that you can avoid the grief through a type of negotiation. If you change this, I'll change that. You are so desperate to get your life back to how it was before the grief event, you are willing to make a major life change in an attempt toward normality. Guilt is a common wing man of bargaining. This is when you endure the endless "what if" statements. What if I had left the house 5 minutes sooner – the accident would have never happened. What if I encouraged him to go to the doctor six months ago like I first thought – the cancer could have been found sooner and he could have been saved.

Depression

Depression is a commonly accepted form of grief. In fact, most people associate depression immediately with grief – as it is a "present" emotion. It represents the emptiness we feel when we are living in reality and realize the person or situation is gone or over. In this stage, you might withdraw from life, feel numb, live in a fog, and not want to get out of bed. The world might seem too much and too overwhelming for you to face. You don't want to be around others, don't feel like talking, and experience feelings of hopelessness. You might even experience suicidal thoughts – thinking "what's the point of going on?"

Acceptance

The last stage of grief identified by Kübler-Ross is acceptance. Not in the sense that "it's okay my husband died" rather, "my husband died, but I'm going to be okay." In this stage, your emotions may begin to stabilize. You re-enter reality. You come to terms with the fact that the "new" reality is that your partner is never coming back – or that you are going to succumb to your illness and die soon – and you're okay with that. It's not a "good" thing – but it's something you can live with. It is definitely a time of adjustment and readjustment. There are good days, there are bad days, and then there are good days again. In this stage, it does not mean you'll never have another bad day – where you are uncontrollably sad. But, the good days tend to outnumber the bad days. In this stage, you may lift from your fog, you start to engage with friends again, and might even make new relationships as time goes on. You understand your loved one can never be replaced, but you move, grow, and evolve into your new reality.

https://www.psycom.net/depression.central.grief.html

8.1. Forgiveness

After grief comes forgiveness. At times, these happen can be simultaneous. First, you need to forgive yourself and then the other person. Healing starts with forgiving. Forgiving is not a feeling, it's a choice.

Second you need to be patient with yourself. Because we think we can rush into continuing with our lives like nothing ever happened. But hey, believe me you are not okay yet. It's like you have had a big surgery, and you can't go running 50 miles or climb the Kilimanjaro. Well, you could, it sounds like fun. But you get my point. After this big event in your life, you need to heal, and that process takes time. You need to take your time.

Take responsibility for your life. Self-Accountability. This is powerful. This helped me! When you take the responsibility of your life back in your hands, miracles happen. Working hard on yourself and finding yourself back. It's very important how you see yourself. Do you see yourself as a victim or a victor? I want you to switch fast from the victim point of view to that of a victor. That's how you get your power back, and you are then taking responsibility for your life back.

Tell yourself this: The things that happened weren't nice at all, it is what it is, but I will now continue with my life and take full responsibility to make it better and learn from this experience.

The faster you can accept the situation as it is, the easier you can move on with your life.

Third: don't jump into any relationship yet. Because you will then go with your past hurts into the next relationship, and this won't do the relationship any good.

Fourth; and this is my favorite, I suggest you cry a lot. Crying heals your soul. I suggest you journal about your emotions and whatever crosses your mind. Be aware of those negative thoughts, write them down and afterward you can analyze them. Write about what happened, this is a therapy for yourself. Writing or journaling as they call it now a days, is a tool for healing.

Simultaneously search for a professional help from a psychologist or a coach. After I jumped with my parachute, I went to a psychologist who helped me very well and I went to a "Heal your life" course by Louise Hay. If there is no course around in your city, you can read the book and buy the workbook so you can do the assignments. You can also go to a coach to help you guide you. I heard that TaMi Coaching is awesome. You can try her😊

"The heal your life" course by Louise Hay, was one of the turning points in my journey. It helped me look into my life and note the areas that needed to be healed and restored. Because when you are healing and discovering yourself, you come to see areas of your life that aren't good at all. There may be things you need to change in yourself.

Like setting healthy boundaries, loving yourself and respect yourself. Those things weren't in place at all. I lacked in all those areas. At this moment in your life, you realize that because you didn't have some things straight you allowed certain things to happen to you. Because you were also lacking in some areas. Now you feel like I'm blaming you. No, that's not the point and I'm not. But you need to work on yourself otherwise this could happen to you again. If you don't love and respect yourself and you don't have any boundaries, how can you stand up for yourself next time? So read on and you will get it.

Ta Mi Bida!

Chapter 9 - Finding yourself back. The road to self-discovery.

After the healing process and this takes time. I cannot say exactly how long. For everybody it's different. It took me about two years, to really heal.

Then the road to self-discovery starts. I think they go together. Because the healing and the awareness are also part of your self-discovery.

When I left, I started to look for answers. I always liked reading books, but I forgot I did, or I didn't feel like reading at that time. I went to my library, and I was looking for an answer. And then I found this book titled "The one". I thought the book was going to tell me who 'The one', was. To my surprise 'the one' was talking about God and God in you. So 'the one' was more about relying on and loving yourself.

Pffffffft what a disappointment. I wanted answers. But I continued reading the book. And I started understanding the message. The bottom line of this book was that everything starts and ends with you. You need to first love yourself, believe in yourself and guess what?

Yes, you are the only one who can do this. You must partake in your own rescue. Off course you need professional help, but most of the work you will do for yourself. Nobody is going to rescue you.

Then all these questions started popping up:

Who am I? What do I want in life?

What are my talents? What are my interests?

What do I like?

By asking these questions you are digging deep into who you really are. Because you forgot who you were. You need to find your identity back.

We let society dictate how we need to be and behave. Then we tell ourselves also a bunch of lies by the negative beliefs and thoughts we have about ourselves and we forget our true "Soul Path". Finding your Ikigai is the ultimate quest in your life. In the last chapter I will tell you what the Ikigai is and where it leads you to.

Chapter 10 - Gaining Self-Confidence Self-Love Back

Go and love yourself. Many times, I hear coaches (and I'm a coach too hahaha) and in the past my friends did say to me, love yourself more. Okay, great! How do I do that?

What is self-love? Self-care is self-love. And self-care comes with different aspects.

First, taking care of yourself. Have enough rest, me-time, mindfulness, do some exercise, eat well. Those are some self-care tips.

Secondly, setting healthy boundaries is self-care. How do you set healthy boundaries? By saying no, when you can't without feeling guilty. Evaluate if you want to do something yes or no. Don't be a people pleaser just to please others and you are putting too much on your plate.

Self-care is also loving yourself. If you love yourself, you respect yourself and you wouldn't take s&^% from anyone.

Some practices you can do is look yourself in the mirror, look in your eyes and tell yourself that you love yourself. It will feel weird at first and maybe even difficult to do at first. But try to do it every day. Write it on a post-it note "I'm enough", stick it on your mirror or somewhere you see it every day. You are enough means that you are complete, you have everything in you to be enough, to be resourceful etc.

How can you gain more self-confidence? The way we speak and think of ourselves determines how we see ourselves. Self-image. So always speak and think empowering things to yourself. Use affirmations: "I'm beautiful, I'm capable, I have everything in me to be successful, I'm blessed, I'm smart' etc. etc.

Self-confidence is a skill. This means you can learn this, by taking courageous action steps. Every time you step out of your comfort zone and do something that scares you, you are working on that self-confidence muscle.

We behave exactly how we believe we are. You also need to question your belief system. What is your belief system? All the things that you believe is true to you, but some are lies you told yourself. These beliefs come from 1. Your parents, 2. Your peers, 3. Society and 4. You also told yourself a few.

Some beliefs don't work in your advantage. A believe can be e.g. "I'm not creative, I'm not a morning person, I'm not good at sports, I can't learn technology" etc. etc. You get my point.

These beliefs you probably heard them somewhere or you saw it or experienced some sort of event and then you concluded this belief. Where did you come up with this belief? Go back in your childhood or young adolescence and think about it!

These beliefs do not serve you at all! Question them and be very critical about them. And then rewrite these beliefs. Write a new story and make some new set of beliefs that can serve you better.

Be very aware of your thoughts. One powerful tool that helped me so much in my life is journaling. By writing all your thoughts on paper, you can make the unconscious, conscious. And when you are conscious and aware of what you are thinking, you can then change the way you think.

And with more awareness, you can make better choices and with better choices you get better results.

10.1 Self-help books

Read a lot of self-development and self-help books. One must-read about self-care is "The Art of Extreme Self-Care" by Cheryl Richardson. Some other books like "The 4 Agreements" by Don Miguel Ruiz speaks about the belief system and other agreements we can use in our lives. Books by John Maxwell and Valory Burton, Tony Robbins are a few of my favorites. And the book by Louise Hay: "You Can Heal your Life". For books about spirituality and other topics, I refer you to Wayne Dyer.

Please take time to read at least 10 pages every day. When you read a few books, a few light bulbs are going to light up in your head. And that's a good thing. Then you are going to find out even more who you really are. Then you are ready to peel off the layers of who you are NOT.

More on this topic in the next chapter. Read on….

Chapter 11 - Living Aligned to who you truly are.

Who are you?

This question is powerful. Ask yourself what do you like? What are some of your strengths and what are some of your weaknesses? What are your values? What do you tolerate and what not? What do you stand for? What is your life's philosophy? Who are you?

After you did good research on yourself you have to live by it and never ever settle for less. Then you can live a life true to yourself.

We are so conditioned to live our lives to what others might think of us and we forget who we really are.

Ask yourself these questions every day: Am I my truest self, right now? What do I want more of in my life so I can be more authentic? What do I NOT want more of in my life so I can be authentic?

11.1 Quitting the people pleasing.

I used to try to please everybody and still until this day it's difficult for me not to do so. Because I like to help others and I go out of my way to please everybody. But I learned this the hard way. Now I put myself first. This is not selfish, it's self-first.

One book that helped me on this topic was: "The subtle art of not giving a f&^%."

Why are we such people pleasers? Do you know the answer? Let me tell you about it. Many women were raised to please others. And for some parents, it is even an educational goal for their daughters. As woman, we are often reminded to please the man, we need to do everything in the house. Please the man so he is happy with you and won't look for another woman. Say what!!!!!!!!!!!!!!! Are you kidding me? It feels like slavery and/or feels like the man can replace us anytime. What is this philosophy? We are not less than men. On the contrary, the man needs to honor us, and treat us well.

Ladies we are gems! Believe this and live by it. And I hear you thinking, yeah right, I am a gem, but I don't feel this way, how can I believe this and feel more like this?

First, we were created as equals to men. If we look in the bible, God made us equal to men and he took a piece of his rib to make us. And furthermore, without a woman there would be no more generations. Isn't that enough evidence that we are worth a lot? We are the apple of God's eye.

I can tell you all of these things, but you need to believe it. Write down your statement or your mantra. Every time you doubt yourself read this out loud twice! Once in the morning, once at night.

11.2 Setting boundaries.

When I met my current husband, I was quite harsh on setting boundaries. Remember, I went from a place of no boundaries at all, to a place of stepping up for myself. Yes, you guessed it, I went a little bit Godzilla on him. I told him this: "I'm not ironing your clothes, I don't like household tasks, and I won't cook for you every day. Take it or leave it."

He stared at me for a few seconds, I could see him thinking like what the hell?! He then said to my surprise: "okay!" I was in shock that he respected my boundaries and that he was okay with it.

But then he replied. He said: "I don't mind, the only thing I want is peace of mind". I'm like okay, that's easy breezy, I can do that. But then I thought, wait, what does he mean by peace of mind? And then he explained to me.

It's very important to ask questions. Not assuming things. Because peace of mind means something to me, but it could mean something entirely different for him.

So going back to this story. I was harsh in the beginning. But it changed throughout the years. I just ended a relationship, where I was fed up and where I had no boundaries at all. And now I wanted to put clear boundaries like they were written in mortar.

Of course, after some time when everything seems to go nice between us, I started to do more for him. It's important in a relationship that there is reciprocity. It's about giving and taking and there should be a balance.

The problem here is this. Because we never set healthy boundaries, we don't really know how to set them in a correct way. We are not assertive yet. We become a little aggressive when it comes to boundaries. Why? Because we go from one extreme to the other. We have to first learn how to set it, without getting emotional or angry. We can say it kindly. You don't have to be aggressive or bold so that the other person can understand it. Well sometimes! Some people don't understand in the nice way, really!

But in general, try to set boundaries and be assertive. Like: thanks for asking me, but I will not be able to make it. Or 'I didn't like the way you said x, y, z, I appreciate that you did x, y,z'.

You see! You can set boundaries without getting aggressive or emotional. But this takes practice.

Oh, and another very important thing about this. You always did everything for everybody and now you don't? You are now setting boundaries, that before you didn't. People will not recognize you and will start wondering what happened to you. You've changed. Logically because you were always so compliant and with no boundaries, people will start to withdraw from your life once you set boundaries. And that's ok. Because these people were using you and they don't respect you. So let them go.

The ones that love and respect you, will understand and respect your boundaries.

11.3: Be yourself! Be authentic.

The essence of everything is to live a life true to yourself. One that you can live authentically to who you are. It is so important to be yourself. In a world where copycats and society norms are the norm, we need to be ourselves and stick to what we believe and stick to what is good for us.

Be yourself. Live authentically.

How does one live authentically? Say what you mean and mean what you say! Whatever you do, ask yourself does this feel right in my gut? Is this aligned with who I want to be?

This is not an easy task. The saying: "say what you mean and mean what you say" is not as easy as it seems. But it's liberating. Sometimes people won't like it and sometimes you will even lose some people. But that's okay, too. Because the ones who love you and respect you, will understand. And the ones who don't, let them go. Wish them well and bless them, like I just mentioned before.

Ask yourself every day. Am I being true to myself? Am I the truest to me today? Yes? Great! If not, why not? Ask yourself: "What can I do more of today to be true to myself?"

11.4: Making your own decisions.

Making your own decisions is tough, but also oh so liberating. Your decision to do something in your life, may not please your parents, your friends, or your family. But in the end, it's your life!

If you are not deliberately hurting people or doing mean stuff, you are just choosing to live your life to the beat of your own drum. Do it. For example, you want to live on your own, rent a space, or buy a house. But your parents don't want you to. They try to convince you and sometimes it even feels like they want to manipulate you. You feel bad not making a decision that will please them. But then you feel bad and frustrated and you feel imprisoned. Making your own decisions and sticking to them is liberating.

What freedom you will experience if you choose to go and rent a space anyway so you can be on your own. With love and respect, you tell your parents you really want to do this for your own development, and you wish to get their support and their blessing. If they don't support or bless your decision, do it anyway and you will see! Everything and everybody will come along, eventually.

This isn't selfish, it's self-first.

11.5 Self-actualization.

The humanistic psychologist Maslow and his hierarchy of needs, a.k.a. the pyramid of Maslow.

In his pyramid the last stage is the stage of self-actualization. To give you an idea, the basic needs of any human being are food and sleep. If that stage or level is fulfilled you can move up to the next level, or rather go higher up. To give you a summary of the stages without going too in-depth: the 2nd level is safety needs, the 3rd is love and belonging, 4th is esteem, and the 5th is self-actualization.

The only way you reach the highest level is by developing and learning and finding out who you are and what your talents, gifts and passion are.

In the 5th and last stage of the Pyramid is the self-actualization. When you do the work, you love and do it well and enjoy it and you know who you are, that is when you know you have reached this final stage.

When you get to this stage you will have set your own set of values. Not the ones imposed on you by society, parents, or any other people. You then make your own decisions. And then my beloved sisters, you feel free and aligned to who you really are.

Like the day I found out what my real passion and purpose was, I cried like a baby. I cried tears of happiness that I cannot describe in words. It was one of the happiest days of my life. Like that quote that says there are two days in your life where you are your happiest. That is on the day you were born, and the 2nd is when you know why you were born. This quote is the real deal!!!

When I found out what my Ikigai was, read on to know what that is, my life changed in a rapid tempo.

This was during the lock-down of 2020. When COVID hit, and we all had to stay home. For me this time was a blessing in disguise. More on this in the last chapter.

Ta Mi Bida!

Chapter 12 - Finding your Ikigai (purpose in life).

It was April 2020, and I was at home during the lock down. I didn't really plan to start my coaching's business back then. Before the lock down I was invited to speak at a women's gathering on March 8, women's international day. It was great!!!

To speak to a group of people was one of my goals. And I did! It was so fulfilling. That I thought "okay, I have to do this more often." I want to bring my message of my life's mess and how I turned it around.

After I this, we went into the lockdown. Then I thought, now what?

I was thinking in other ways to still be able to talk with women. I missed my students, because then I was working at school as a teacher and coach.

One day in April I decided to do live streaming on social media. This was my first time ever. I can remember that I was nervous, and I didn't know what to do, but I just hit the "go live" button. From there I continued. I always believed that you need to throw yourself into something and do it. From there you go forth.

There is a beautiful metaphor about this. If the weather is very foggy and you can only see 100 meters in front of you. How can you see the next 100 meters? Can you guess?

You have to walk the first 100 meters, and when you arrive at the 100th meter, you can see the next 100 meters.

It sounds simple, and it is simple. You must take the first step, then the second and the third. And along the way you will have to deal with the challenges. Maybe you will need somebody who is expert on certain areas that you are not. But every step has its assignments. And that's okay. You will get them when you get there. The most important thing to look out for is don't let your fears take over and paralyze you from taking the step.

Excuses: we have tons when it comes to new things. You have to do the things that stretch you out of your comfort zone. Be aware of these excuses. Not one of them is valid. Remember this, reasons come first, answers come second like Tony Robbins says. Don't think about the money that you don't have, or the time you don't have or that the children are small etc. etc.

Reasons come first; answers come second. This means if your 'why' is big enough and you go after it, the answers will automatically come your way.

Like the John Maxwell quote: "Creativity is the joy of not knowing all the answers but of knowing that answers are out there."

As I said before, I wasn't really planning on starting my coaching business during the 2020 lock-down. But it happened. Like I said before in this book, the purpose you are looking for, will eventually find you. You will grow into it. That happened to me. When I was ready and equipped with knowledge and life's experiences, the opportunity came along, and I saw this opportunity and grabbed it.

When preparation meets opportunity that is where the magic happens.

Of course, you have to prepare yourself. Study, read, learn, and work on yourself.

I remember after a few months, somebody told me, you are going fast. How can it be after only a few months that you are doing so well?

I responded; it's not only been a few months. It has taken years of experience, preparation, and late night studies. Fourteen years of preparation, that's not even that much time, but it was enough to take the leap. Of course, the learning process never stops. It keeps growing every day.

When I was pulled towards my purpose, one night I woke up at 1:30 in the morning and started writing all my ideas down and how I saw everything. To me it was like I just had a vision at that moment. I then cried with tears of joy. Because my whole being was aligned. My mind, my heart, my soul, my spirit. I was so blissfully happy. Words can't explain what I felt. I found my purpose!

Now I had to act upon it. I started step by step. With each step I took, I was thinking to not to go back to my job (at school). I couldn't go back. The pull was so strong, that it was pulling me in the direction of my mission and my purpose. I had to leave my paid job.

A lot of people called me crazy for quitting my paid job and starting a business in these difficult times. But let me tell you this. There is no perfect time. There will always be something. If not now, then when? It was one of the best decisions I made in my life.

12.1 What is the soul?

To my opinion your soul is your connection to God, to the universe to the higher power. The soul is your inner strength and voice. The soul knows very well what you want and who you are. But because we don't listen to our soul and we let so many things influence our soul, we forget our soul-path.

What's your soul-path?

Your soul-path knows exactly what makes you happy and what your ultimate passion and mission is on this earth. But we lose our soul-path while we grow up. Because people dictate and influence our soul-path.

Go back to your heart's desire. The one thing that let's your soul shine bright like the sun. What makes you happy? How can you contribute beyond yourself? What are you passionate about? Whom or what do you want to serve?

When you think of purpose, this is always bigger than yourself. It always has to do with others. When you are of service to others. It's not about yourself. You can have different purposes throughout your life. It's not only one big thing to pursue as many might think.

Finding your purpose or like I love the word in Japanese, Ikigai (meaning of life) is not really a quest to something. It's not a quest like in the movie Indiana Jones where the people in the movie are after a treasure.

Well, it is a treasure, don't get me wrong. But it's not something you go after. It will find you. What do I mean?

By developing yourself, learning more about yourself, and developing your gifts and talents and the skillset that belongs to this, you will step into your purpose.

I'm 40 now and a few years ago a good friend of mine told me this: hey you never stay long at a job, do you? I was like huh, I hadn't even thought of it. Now I can think back and realize that I had to do all these different jobs to learn skills and develop myself. I'm indeed somebody that after some time when I've learned everything it becomes automatic. And I don't like that. I like to be challenged and I like new things. After a while the allure of something diminishes. That's one of my character traits. Yes, I have done many personality tests.

But I think also it has to do with the fact that I did like the job, but it wasn't fully what I liked or what I wanted to do for life. It wasn't my purpose. Of course, I had some missions and goals within each job. But it wasn't it. And as I grew, as I developed my talents, gifts, and skills and got to know myself better, I realized I had some beautiful talents, gifts, and skills that I developed over the years.

And when the pandemic hit in 2020, when I was sitting at home, I then realized what my purpose was. As an Educator and teacher, I was always teaching and giving advice. I was good in connecting with people easily. But now the calling was even bigger. I wanted to be an inspiration and give people hope regarding what they could do with their lives. I wanted to coach people, so that they could live a more fulfilling life and find their purpose in life.

12.2 It's my life!

Maybe you're asking yourself, how can I find mine? First, start developing yourself. Learn to know yourself. Discover who you are. What are your weaknesses and what are your strengths? What are your gifts and talents? Develop these. Learn the skillset that belongs to your talent. Grow into it. What do you love to do? Of service of whom you want to be? Why? Does it make you happy and energized? Ask yourself these questions and develop yourself. And your purpose will find you. I think it's not the other way around.

Live authentically and have a happy life aligned to who you really are.

We have now reached the last chapter of this book. And the bottom line is this. The more you can be and live authentically and live by your soul-path and listen to your soul and/or gut, you will be happy. And if you are happy, you will be aligned to who you really are today and always.

Remember "Ta mi Bida", it's my life. It's your life to live. Say it out loud: Ta Mi Bida! It's My Life!

Acknowledgements

My greatest gift in life is the abundance of friends that are always there. My family is small, so God granted me so many good friends that became like family.

Where do I start? I will begin with thanking my mom and dad who are no longer here, but they gave me life. And as I recall every important event in my life they were there on the sideline supporting me and encouraging me. Giving me advice to their best knowledge. I owe them a lot for the woman I am today.

Big lessons learned from them were: "Where there is a will, there is a way", "Never never give up", "If you want something, throw yourself into it" and "God will provide".

Those are a few of the many lessons they taught me.

Second to my husband Rugobert Angel for always supporting me and my crazy ideas. To my daughter Zara, for her patience and love.

Third I want to thank Gisèle Juliet for starting this journey with me. We had this challenge together to write a book simulteanously. She supported me selflessly, throughout my journey. Not only with my book, but throughout my whole journey of starting my business.

To my sister from another mister; Stacy Riding for reviewing my whole book, without hesitation or asking anything in return.

To my cousin Riggwenda Doorjé who was there for me, from day one, supporting me and helping me out selflessly.

To my sisters, Céline Gladpootjes, Rebecca Luis, Cristina Rondon-Vlieg, Giandra Brigitha, Santoshi Ursulita-Lakhi, Denise Leito, Caresse Daal, Shekinah Dare, Monica Badaracco, Yara Yarzagaray, Lyzanne da Costa Gomez, who were very present during this journey.

To my blood brother Andras Erdelyi and my Sister in law Amada Avalos for always sending me books and supporting me in one way or the other. To Feco, I love you too.

To my other brothers: Angelo Davelaar and, Chesley Ocalia.

But never to forget who picked me up back then in those 'dark days' when I was down. Thanks to Tina Ersilia who always listened to me when I was passing through those difficult times. I can not thank you enough to listen to my every call. If I called her 10 times, she would pick up 11 times. To her husband Jurgen Ersilia. You guys are still very special to me.

To all my crazy friends: Las chicas locas. Really you make me laugh and thanks for the support you showed me in one way or the other. I will never forget when I was in Colombia with my sick mother, how you helped me out financially, so I could bring Zara to Colombia with me.

To Inge Boutier who I've learned so much from. Who was there for me since day 1. Thank you! You are family to me. To my fellow coaches: Charlotte Hanst, Chanella Rosalia, Lysandro Inacio. Thank you for your support!

For my new friends who I met along the way, Shahaira & Angelo, Ruth, Roella, Jurinella, Suhainy, Desi, Annie, Karen, Sueene, Sharon, Nella, Gershon, Yithza, and Loise-Ann.

To Tia Eve and Ome Leen for supporting me on every step of my way.

To all my other friends and family who always supported me in one way or the other. They are too many to mention. Please don't take me wrong if I forgot to mention you.

Last but not least, I want to thank all my clients for trusting me to be a support in their lives.

I love you all from the bottom of my heart!

Tami.

Thamara Angel-Erdelyi

Ta Mi Bida!

Ta Mi Bida!

Made in the USA
Middletown, DE
11 March 2022

62436581R00056